Ages 5 and Up

# Alfred's Kid's Electric Guitar Course 1

## The Easiest Electric Guitar Method Ever

**Ron Manus** • **L. C. Harnsberger**

Alfred Music
P.O. Box 10003
Van Nuys, CA 91410-0003
alfred.com

ISBN-10: 1-4706-2384-6 (Book & Online Audio)
ISBN-13: 978-1-4706-2384-5 (Book & Online Audio)

ISBN-10: 1-4706-2404-4 (Book, DVD & Online Audio/Video/Software)
ISBN-13: 978-1-4706-2404-0 (Book, DVD & Online Audio/Video/Software)

*Audio recorded by Jared Meeker.*
*Cover and interior illustrations by Jeff Shelly.*
*Interior photos by Karen Miller and Holly Fraser.*

**Special thanks to our families, friends,
Jared Meeker, Donny Trieu, Robert Hirsh,
Holly Fraser, everyone at Alfred Music, and
Daisy Rock Guitars.**

**Alfred Cares.** Contents printed on
environmentally responsible paper.

# Contents

# Selecting Your Guitar

Guitars come in different types and sizes. It's important to choose a guitar that's just the right size for you, and not one that's too big.

TOO BIG!

Just right.

Guitars come in three basic sizes: 1/2 size, 3/4 size, and full size. You should look and feel comfortable holding your guitar, so it's a good idea to have your local music store's guitar specialist evaluate if your guitar is the right size.

1/2 size     3/4 size     Full-size solid body     Full-size hollow body

## Types of Electric Guitars

**Solid-body** guitars are usually made from a solid piece of wood. They are mostly used to play rock, country, and blues styles.

**Hollow-body** guitars are hollow on the inside of the body. They have a warmer sound than solid-body guitars and are mostly used in jazz, blues, country, and some rock styles.

There's another type of guitar called a **semi-hollow body** that is part solid and part hollow. These guitars have a unique sound and are mainly used for country, blues, and rock music.

3

# Electric Guitars and Amps

## Caring for Your Guitar

Get to know your guitar and treat it like a friend. When you carry it, think of it as part of your body so you don't accidentally bump it against walls or furniture, and be especially sure not to drop it! Every time you're done playing, carefully dust off your guitar with a soft cloth, and put it away in its case.

## The Amplifier

The amplifier (or amp) makes the sound of a guitar louder and lets you add effects to your sound like distortion. All amps are different, but here are a few features you will find on virtually every amp.

**Input Jack**: This is where you plug in your guitar.

**Drive Select**: Activates the Drive channel.

**Drive Volume**: Controls the loudness of the Drive channel.

**Headphone Jack**: Plug in your mono or stereo headphones.

**Power Switch**: This switch turns the amp ON and OFF.

**Reverb**: Reverb adds an echo sound to your playing. Not all amps have this feature.

**Speaker**: The sound comes directly out of the amp through the speaker. Be careful not to touch the speaker because it can be easily damaged.

**Tone Controls**: You can adjust the high (treble), middle, and low (bass) sounds of your guitar. Use these controls to find a sound you like.

**Volume**: The higher the number, the louder the sound. Be aware of who is around you before turning up the volume.

**To start out, set your amp to a comfortable volume with the drive off and the tone set to the middle settings (not high or low).**

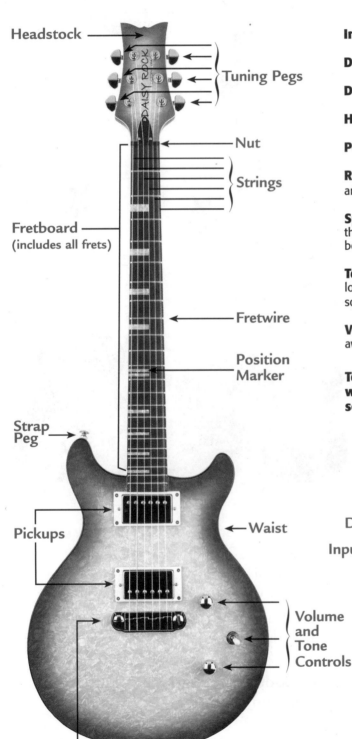

Headstock

Tuning Pegs

Nut

Strings

Fretboard (includes all frets)

Fretwire

Position Marker

Strap Peg

Pickups

Waist

Volume and Tone Controls

Bridge

Strap Peg

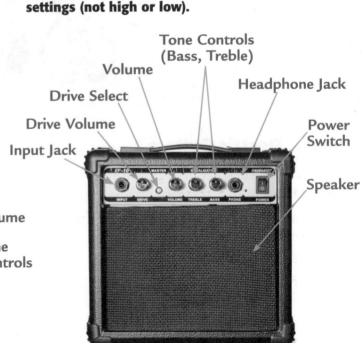

Tone Controls (Bass, Treble)

Volume

Drive Select

Drive Volume

Input Jack

Headphone Jack

Power Switch

Speaker

# Tuning Your Guitar

First make sure your strings are wound properly around the tuning pegs. They should go from the inside to the outside, as in the picture. Some guitars have all six tuning pegs on the same side of the headstock, and in this case make sure all six strings are wound the same way, from inside out.

Turning a tuning peg clockwise makes the pitch lower. Turning a tuning peg counter-clockwise makes the pitch higher. Be sure not to tune the strings too high because they could break!

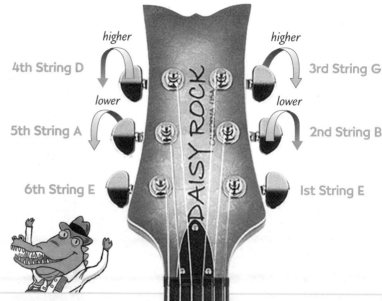

## Important:

Always remember that the thinnest, highest-sounding string, the one closest to the floor, is the 1st string. The thickest, lowest-sounding string, the one closest to the ceiling, is the 6th string. When guitarists say "the highest string," they mean the highest sounding string.

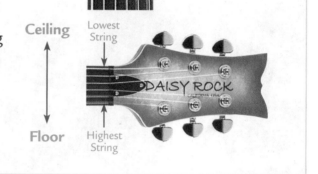

## Tuning with the Audio Tracks  Tracks 1 & 2

### Using Audio Tracks
Access the online audio with a computer or mobile device (see inside front cover) and play Tracks 1 and 2. Listen to the directions and match each of your guitar's strings to its pitch on the audio tracks.

### Using the Video
Tuning Tracks 1 and 2 are also available with the accompanying video. They're available as MP3 files in the DVD-ROM Materials folder on the disc as well as being embedded in the TNT 2 player included with the DVD or as a download. To find the video lesson on tuning in the DVD menu, look for the chapter titled Tuning Your Guitar.

## Tuning without the Audio Tracks or Video

### Tuning the Guitar to Itself
When your 6th string is in tune, you can tune the rest of the strings just using the guitar alone. First, tune the 6th string to E on the piano, then follow the instructions to the right to get the guitar in tune.

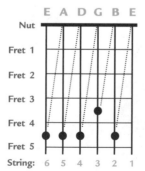

Press 5th fret of 6th string to get pitch of 5th string (A).

Press 5th fret of 5th string to get pitch of 4th string (D).

Press 5th fret of 4th string to get pitch of 3rd string (G).

Press 4th fret of 3rd string to get pitch of 2nd string (B).

Press 5th fret of 2nd string to get pitch of 1st string (E).

## Pitch Pipes and Electronic Tuners
If you don't have a piano available, buying an electronic tuner or pitch pipe is recommended. The salesperson at your music store can show you how to use them.

# How to Hold Your Guitar

Hold your guitar in the position that is most comfortable for you.

Some positions are shown below.

**Sitting with guitar on left leg**

**Sitting with guitar on right leg**

**Standing with strap**

# Strumming the Strings

To *strum* means to play the strings with your right hand by brushing quickly across them. There are two common ways of strumming the strings. One is with your fingers, and the other is with a pick.

## Strumming with a Pick

Hold the pick between your thumb and index finger. Hold it firmly, but don't squeeze it too hard.

Strum from the 6th string (the thickest, lowest-sounding string) to the 1st string (the thinnest, highest-sounding string).

Start near the 6th string.

Move mostly your wrist, not just your arm. Finish near the 1st string.

## Strumming with Your Fingers

First decide if you feel more comfortable strumming with the side of your thumb or the nail of your index finger. The strumming motion is the same with the thumb or finger as it is when using the pick. Strum from the 6th string (the thickest, lowest-sounding string) to the 1st string (the thinnest, highest-sounding string).

Strumming with the thumb

Strumming with the index finger

### Important:

Strum by mostly moving your wrist, not just your arm. Use as little motion as possible. Start as close to the top string as you can, and never let your hand move past the edge of the guitar.

## Time to Strum!  Track 3

Strum all six strings slowly and evenly.

Count your strums out loud as you play.

Repeat this exercise until you feel comfortable strumming the strings.

| | strum | strum | strum | strum | strum | strum | strum | strum |
|---|---|---|---|---|---|---|---|---|
| | / | / | / | / | / | / | / | / |
| Count: | 1 | 2 | 3 | 4 | 5 | 6 | 7 | 8 |

# Strumming Notation

## Beats

Each strum you play is equal to one *beat*. Beats are even, like the ticking of a clock.

tick - tick - tick - tick
beat - beat - beat - beat

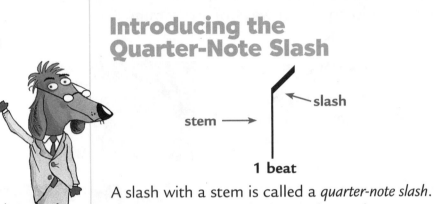

### Introducing the Quarter-Note Slash

slash

stem →

**1 beat**

A slash with a stem is called a *quarter-note slash*. Each quarter-note slash equals one beat.

## The Staff and Treble Clef

Guitar music is usually written on a five-line *staff* that has a *treble clef* at its beginning.

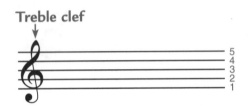

Treble clef

5
4
3
2
1

## Bar Lines, Measures, and Time Signatures

*Bar lines* divide the staff into equal parts called *measures*. A *double bar line* is used at the end to show you the music is finished.

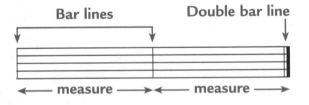

Bar lines     Double bar line

← measure → ← measure →

Measures are always filled with a certain number of beats. You know how many beats are in each measure by looking at the *time signature*, which is always at the beginning of the music. A $\frac{4}{4}$ time signature ("four-four time") means there are four equal beats in every measure.

Time signature

## More Time to Strum  Track 4

Play this example in $\frac{4}{4}$ time. It will sound the same as "Time to Strum," which you played on the previous page. Keep the beats even and count out loud.

**First time:** Strum all six strings as you did before.

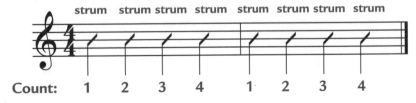

strum  strum strum  strum   strum  strum strum  strum

Count:     1      2      3      4      1      2      3      4

**Second time:** Strum starting with the 3rd string, and strum only strings 3, 2, and 1.

Strumming strings 3–2–1

# Using Your Left Hand

## Hand Position

Learning to use your left-hand fingers easily starts with a good hand position. Place your hand so your thumb rests comfortably in the middle of the back of the neck. Position your fingers on the front of the neck as if you are gently squeezing a ball between them and your thumb. Keep your elbow in and your fingers curved.

Keep elbow in and fingers curved

Like gently squeezing a ball between your fingertips and thumb

## Placing a Finger on a String

When you press a string with a left-hand finger, make sure you press firmly with the tip of your finger and as close to the fretwire as you can without actually being right on it. Short fingernails are important! This will create a clean, bright tone.

**RIGHT**
Finger presses the string down near the fret without actually being on it.

**WRONG**
Finger is too far from fretwire; tone is "buzzy" and indefinite.

**WRONG**
Finger is on top of fretwire; tone is muffled and unclear.

## How to Read Chord Diagrams

Chord diagrams show where to place your fingers. The example to the right shows finger 1 on the 1st string at the 1st fret. The Xs above the 6th, 5th and 4th strings tell you not to play them and only strum the 3rd, 2nd and 1st strings. Strings that are not played in a chord also look like dashed lines. The os above the 2nd and 3rd strings tell you these strings are to be played *open,* meaning without pressing down on them with a left-hand finger.

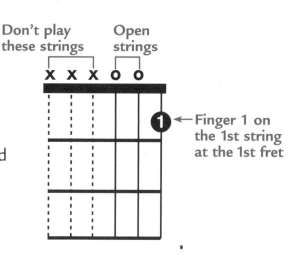

Don't play these strings

Open strings

X X X O O

1 ← Finger 1 on the 1st string at the 1st fret

9

# The Three-String C Chord

**Hear this chord!**

Track 5

Use finger 1 to press the 2nd string at the 1st fret.
Strum strings 3–2–1.

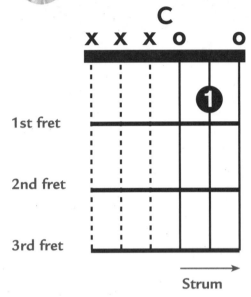

Strum

Track 6

## Strumming

Strum the three-string C chord on each quarter-note slash . Make sure your strums are even. Count aloud as you play:

**1–2–3–4 | 1–2–3–4**

Listen to the song to hear how it should sound!

# My First Chord

Remember: This means there are four beats in each measure.

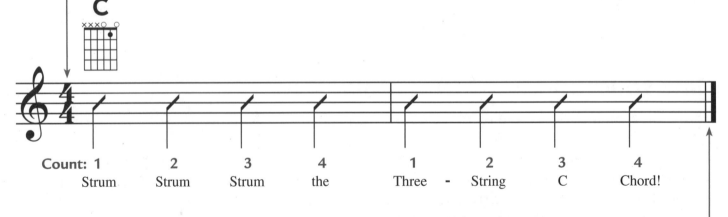

| Count: 1 | 2 | 3 | 4 | 1 | 2 | 3 | 4 |
|---|---|---|---|---|---|---|---|
| Strum | Strum | Strum | the | Three | - String | C | Chord! |

This **double bar** line tells us the music is finished.

# The Quarter Rest

## Introducing the Quarter Rest

This strange-looking music symbol means to be silent for one beat. Stop the sound of the strings by lightly touching them with the side of your hand, as in the photo.

1 beat

Track 7

### Rest Warm-up

Before playing "Three Blind Mice," practice this exercise until you are comfortable playing rests.

strum strum strum [stop]   strum strum strum [stop]

1    2    3    (rest)    1    2    3    (rest)

## Practice Tip

Strum the chords and have a friend sing the words.

# Three Blind Mice

Track 8   C

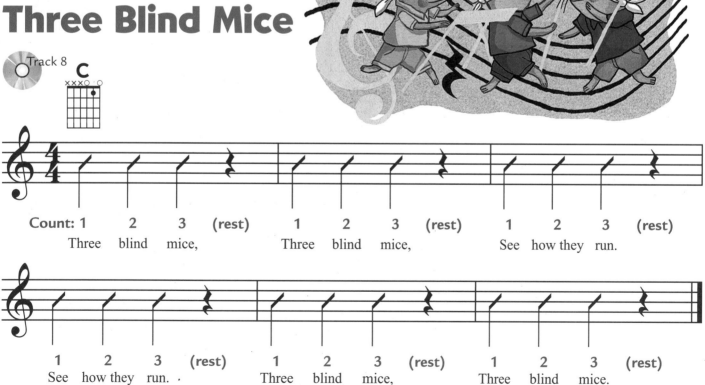

Count: 1    2    3    (rest)    1    2    3    (rest)    1    2    3    (rest)
Three blind mice,    Three blind mice,    See how they run.

1    2    3    (rest)    1    2    3    (rest)    1    2    3    (rest)
See how they run.    Three blind mice,    Three blind mice.

# The Three-String G⁷ Chord

Use finger 1 to press the 1st string at the 1st fret.

Strum strings 3–2–1.

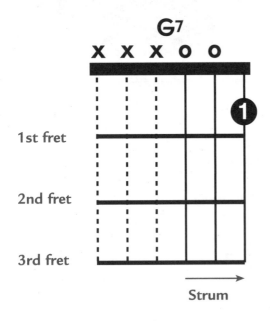

## My Second Chord

Track 10

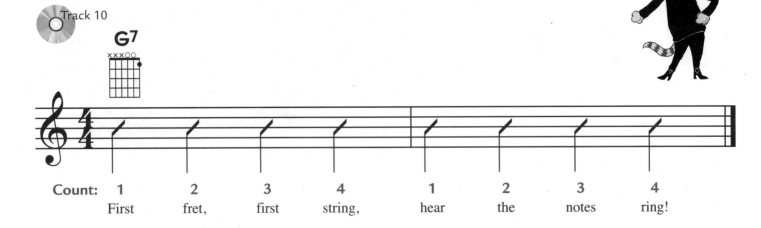

| Count: | 1 | 2 | 3 | 4 | 1 | 2 | 3 | 4 |
|--------|---|---|---|---|---|---|---|---|
| | First | fret, | first | string, | hear | the | notes | ring! |

12

# Troubadour Song

Remember to stop the sound by lightly touching the strings with the side of your hand on each ‚. Wait one beat.

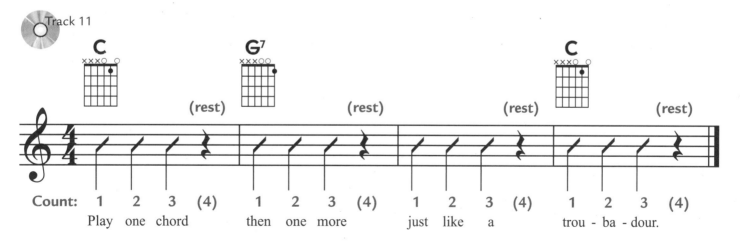

Track 11

| C | G⁷ | C |

Count: 1 2 3 (4)   1 2 3 (4)   1 2 3 (4)   1 2 3 (4)

Play one chord   then one more   just like a   trou - ba - dour.

*A troubadour was a musician who traveled around singing and playing.

# Skip to My Lou

**G⁷**

**C**

## Practice Tip

To change quickly from G⁷ to C in the last two measures, just move your finger from the 1st string to the 2nd string—that's not very far.

Track 12

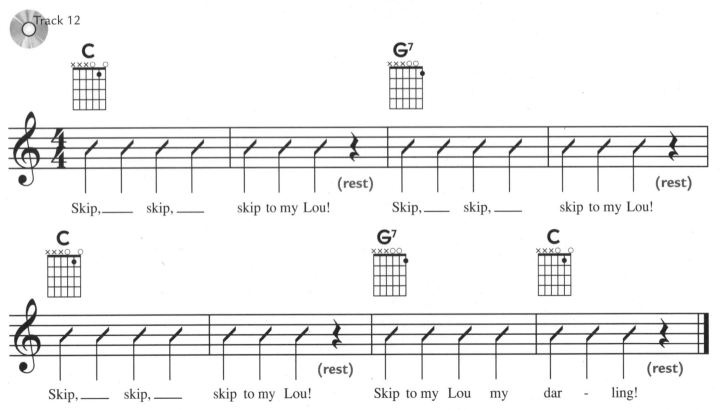

Skip,____ skip,____ skip to my Lou! Skip,____ skip,____ skip to my Lou!

Skip,____ skip,____ skip to my Lou! Skip to my Lou my dar - ling!

# London Bridge

Track 13

C         G⁷         C

Lon - don Bridge is   fal - ling down,    (rest)    fal - ling down,    (rest)    fal - ling down    (rest)

(No new chord symbol, so keep playing C!)     G⁷     C

Lon - don Bridge is   fal - ling down,    (rest)    my____ fair____ la - dy.    (rest)

Remember to move your 1st finger quickly back to the 2nd string to play the C chord on the next beat.

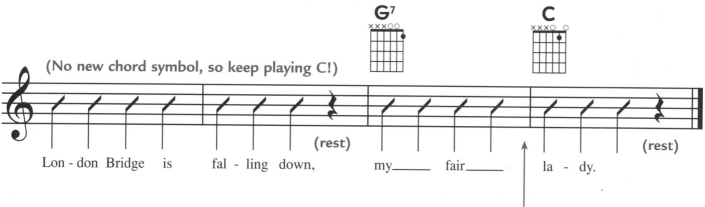

15

# The Three-String G Chord

**Hear this chord!** Track 14

Use finger 3 to press the 1st string at the 3rd fret. Strum strings 3–2–1.

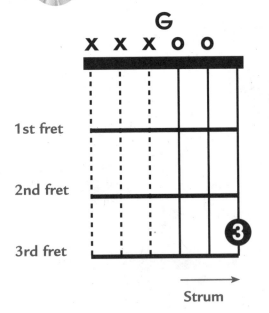

## My Third Chord

Track 15

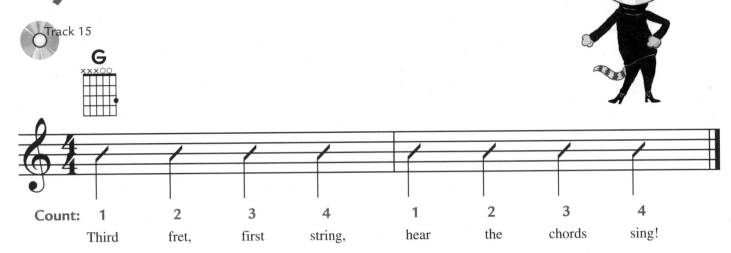

| Count: | 1 | 2 | 3 | 4 | 1 | 2 | 3 | 4 |
|---|---|---|---|---|---|---|---|---|
| | Third | fret, | first | string, | hear | the | chords | sing! |

# Three Chords in One Song

| C | G⁷ | G |
|---|---|---|
|  |  | 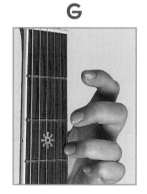 |

## Rain Comes Down

Track 16

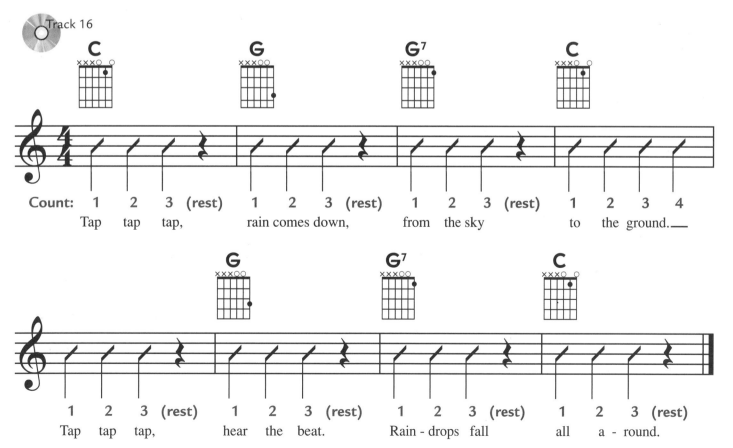

Count: 1 2 3 (rest) 1 2 3 (rest) 1 2 3 (rest) 1 2 3 4
Tap tap tap, rain comes down, from the sky to the ground.

1 2 3 (rest) 1 2 3 (rest) 1 2 3 (rest) 1 2 3 (rest)
Tap tap tap, hear the beat. Rain - drops fall all a - round.

17

# The Repeat Sign

## Introducing the Repeat Sign :‖

Double dots on the inside of a double bar line mean to go back to the beginning and play again.

# Merrily We Roll Along

Track 17

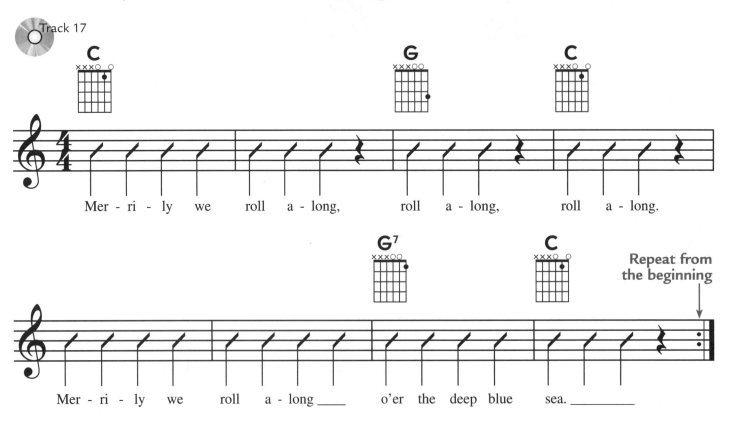

C · G · C

Mer - ri - ly we roll a - long, roll a - long, roll a - long.

G⁷ · C

Repeat from the beginning

Mer - ri - ly we roll a - long ____ o'er the deep blue sea. ____

18

# Love Somebody

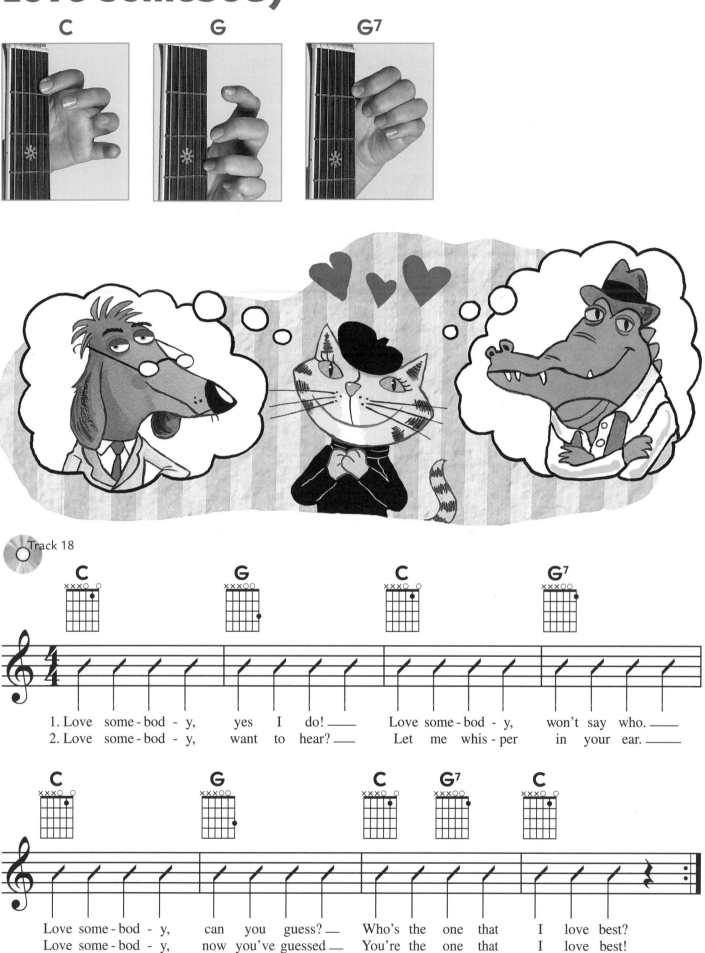

# The Three-String D⁷ Chord

Hear this chord! Track 19

Use finger 1 to press the 2nd string at the 1st fret. Use fingers 2 and 3 to press the 3rd and 1st strings at the 2nd fret.

Strum strings 3–2–1.

**D⁷**

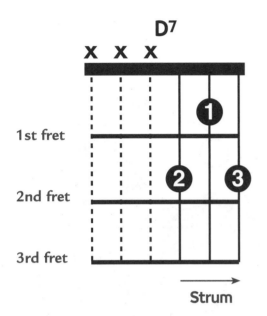

**Strum**

# My Fourth Chord

Track 20

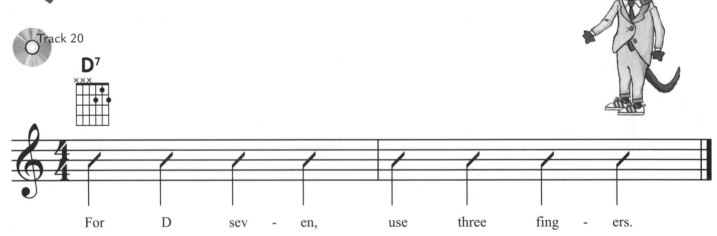

For D sev - en, use three fing - ers.

# Using D⁷ with Other Chords

## Practice Tip

Before you play "When the Saints Go Marching In" and "Yankee Doodle," practice the exercises on this page. They will help you to change chords easily.

Play each exercise very slowly at first, and gradually play them faster. Don't move on to the songs until you can easily move from chord to chord without missing a beat.

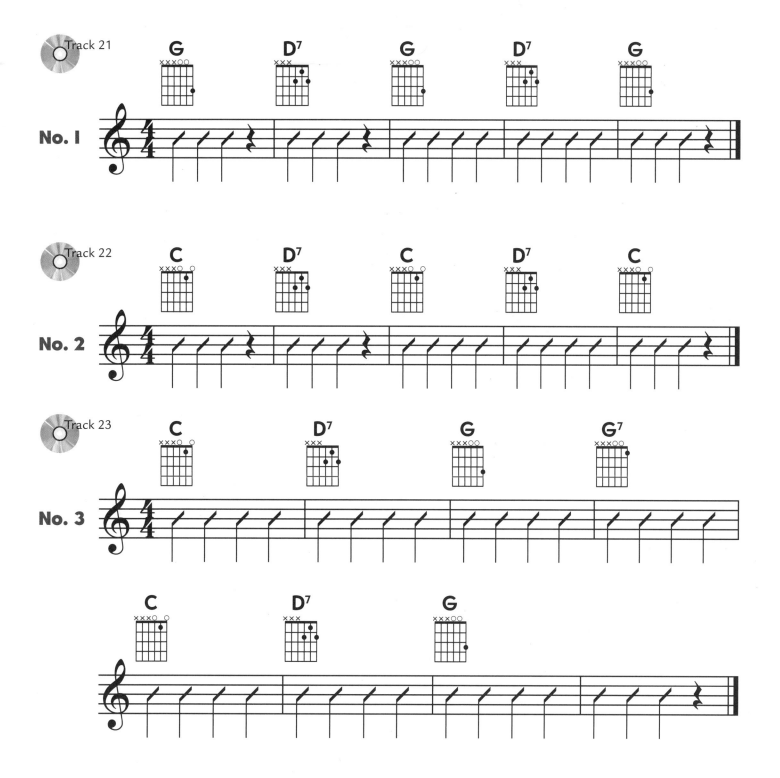

21

# When the Saints Go Marching In

Have some fun and turn on the drive on your amp to use a distorted sound on this song and others throughout the book.

Track 24

# Yankee Doodle

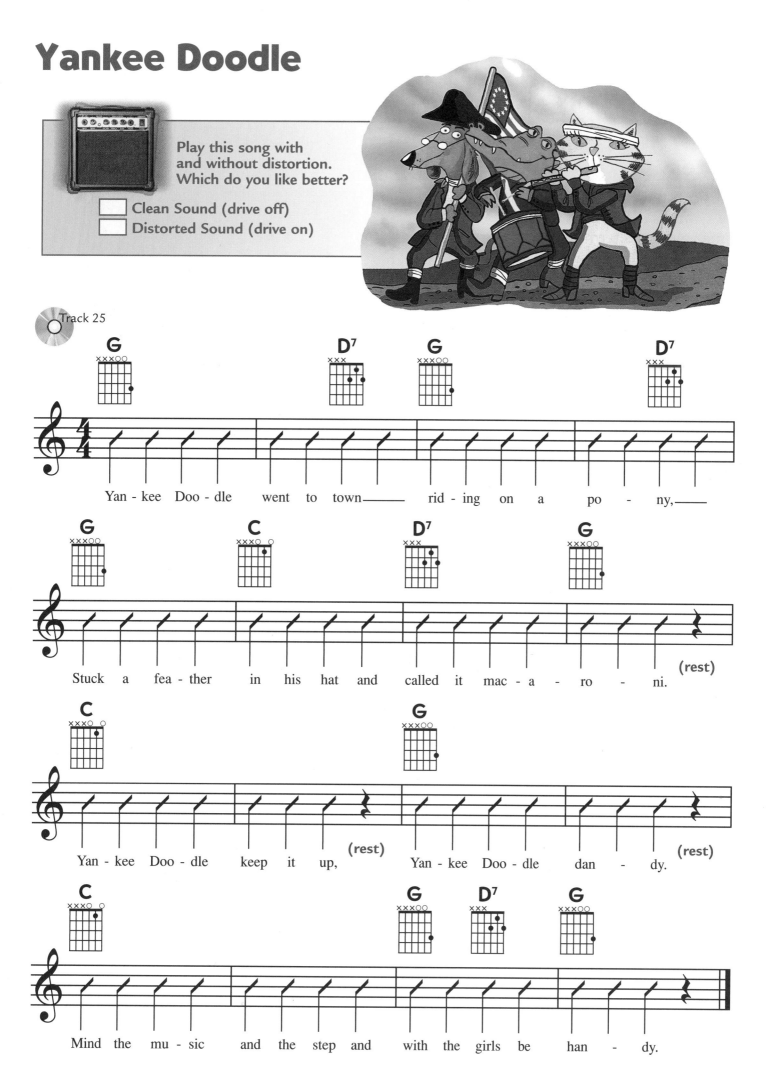

Play this song with
and without distortion.
Which do you like better?

☐ Clean Sound (drive off)
☐ Distorted Sound (drive on)

Track 25

**G** **D⁷** **G** **D⁷**

Yan - kee Doo - dle went to town —— rid - ing on a po - ny, ——

**G** **C** **D⁷** **G**

Stuck a fea - ther in his hat and called it mac - a - ro - ni. **(rest)**

**C** **G**

Yan - kee Doo - dle keep it up, **(rest)** Yan - kee Doo - dle dan - dy. **(rest)**

**C** **G** **D⁷** **G**

Mind the mu - sic and the step and with the girls be han - dy.

23

# Getting Acquainted with Music Notation

## Notes

Musical sounds are represented by symbols called *notes*. Their time value is determined by their color (black or white), and by stems and flags attached to them.

## The Staff

Each note has a name. That name depends on where the note is found on the *staff*. The staff is made up of five horizontal lines and the spaces between those lines.

```
————————————————— 5th LINE —————————————————
                                                      4th SPACE
————————————————— 4th LINE —————————————————
                                              3rd SPACE
————————————————— 3rd LINE —————————————————
                                      2nd SPACE
————————————————— 2nd LINE —————————————————
                              1st SPACE
— 1st LINE —————————————————————————————————
```

## The Music Alphabet

The notes are named after the first seven letters of the alphabet (A–G).

A    B    C    D    E    F    G

## Clefs

As music notation progressed through history, the staff had from two to twenty lines, and symbols were invented that would always give you a reference point for all the other notes. These symbols were called *clefs*.

Music for the guitar is written in the G or *treble clef*. Originally, the Gothic letter G was used on a four-line staff to show the pitch G.

This developed into the modern clef:

An easy way to remember the notes on the lines is using the phrase **E**very **G**ood **B**ird **D**oes **F**ly. Remembering the notes in the spaces is even easier because they spell the word **FACE**, which rhymes with "space."

| Notes on the lines | Notes in the spaces |
|---|---|
| E G B D F | F A C E |

## Introducing the Quarter Note

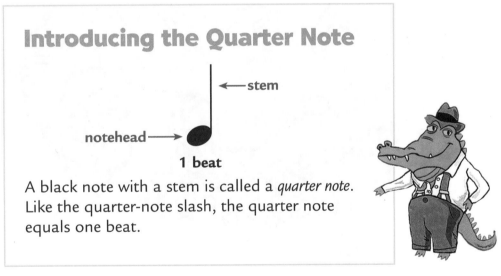

stem

notehead →

**1 beat**

A black note with a stem is called a *quarter note*. Like the quarter-note slash, the quarter note equals one beat.

Track 26

# Clap and Count out Loud

1  2  3  4   1  2  3  (4)   1  2  3  (4)   1  2  3  (4)

# Notes on the First String
# Introducing E

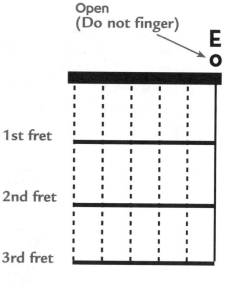
Open
(Do not finger)

E
O

1st fret

2nd fret

3rd fret

**Hear this note!**
Track 27

A note sitting on the top space of the treble clef staff is called E. To play this note, pick the *open* 1st string (meaning without putting a left-hand finger on it).

# Elizabeth, the Elephant

## Picking

- Play each E slowly and evenly, using a *downpick* motion. We will use only downpicks for the rest of Book 1.
- Use only a little motion to pick each note, just like strumming.

Track 28

Count: 1   2   3   4    1   2   3   4    1   2   3   4    1   2   3   4

El - e - phants eat    en - chil - a - das,    es - pe - cial - ly    E - li - za - beth.

# The Note E with Chords

## C Chord

## G⁷ Chord

## Practice Tip

For this tune, notice that both the C and $G^7$ chords are fingered with finger 1 at the 1st fret.

Simply move your finger over one string to change chords.

Track 29

### Note and Strum Warm-up

Before playing "Note and Strum," practice this exercise slowly until you are comfortable playing a note followed by a strum.

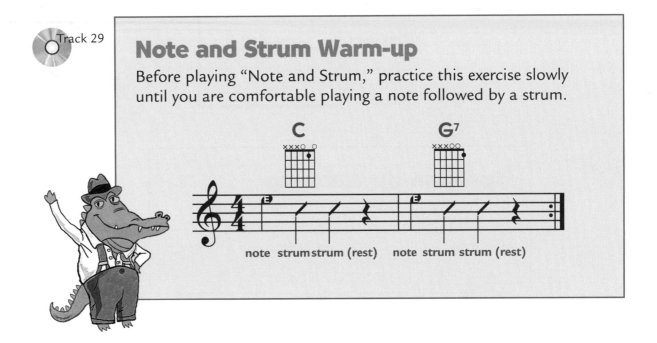

# Note and Strum

Track 30

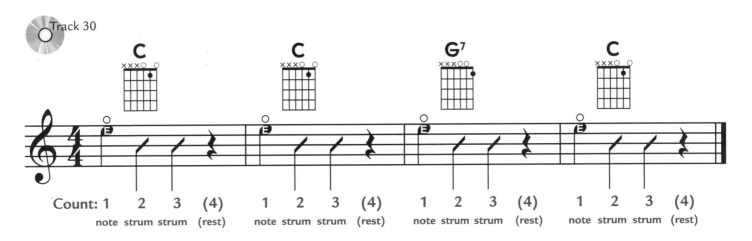

27

# Notes on the First String
# Introducing F

Track 31

A note on the top line of the staff is called F. To play this note, use finger 1 to press the 1st string at the 1st fret. Use a downpick motion to play only the 1st string.

**F**

1st finger

1st fret

2nd fret

3rd fret

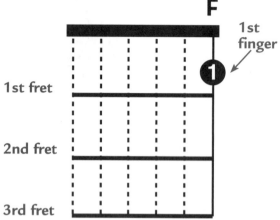

Track 32

## Up-Down-Up Warm-up

Before playing "Up-Down-Up," practice this exercise until you are comfortable playing the note F.

# Up-Down-Up

Track 33

Start on E then up, first fin-ger. Down to E then up to the F.

# The Notes E and F with Chords

## Practice Tip

For this tune, notice that the note F and the G7 chord are both fingered with finger 1 at the 1st fret on the 1st string.

Don't lift your 1st finger between the note F and the G7 chord.

**Note F**   **G⁷ Chord**

Track 34

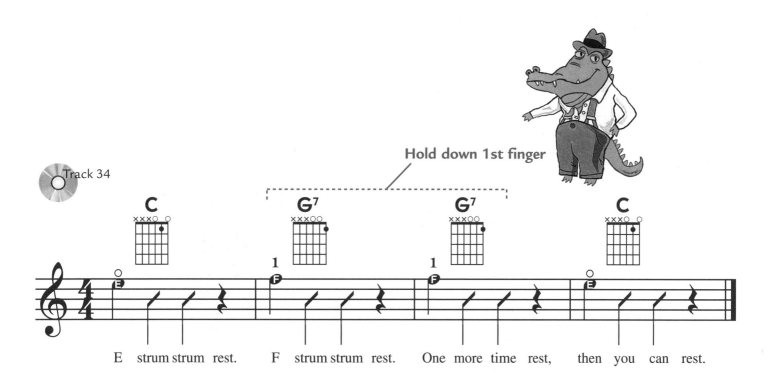

Hold down 1st finger

E strum strum rest.  F strum strum rest.  One more time rest,  then you can rest.

29

# Notes on the First String
# Introducing G

**Hear this note!** Track 35

A note on the space above the staff is called G. Use finger 3 to press the 1st string at the 3rd fret. Use a downpick motion to play only the 1st string.

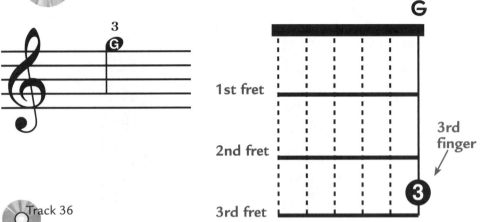

Track 36

## G Warm-up

# The Mountain Climber

Track 37

From the bot - tom to the top, the fear - less climb - er does not stop.

With his pick and tuned gui - tar, the pre - pared climb - er will go far.

30

# The Notes E, F, and G with Chords

### Note G

### G Chord

## Practice Tip

Notice that the note G and the G chord are both fingered with finger 3 at the 3rd fret on the 1st string.

Hold down the 3rd finger between the notes G and the G chord.

## Brave in the Cave

Track 38

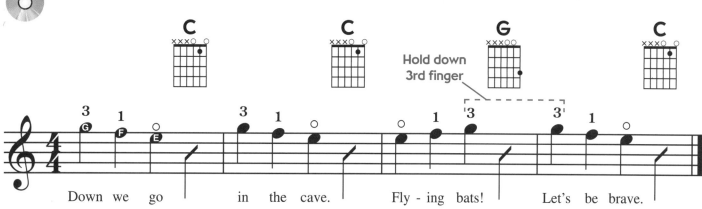

Down we go in the cave. Fly-ing bats! Let's be brave.

31

# Single Notes, Then Chord! Chord! Chord!

Play this song with and without distortion. Which do you like better?

☐ Clean Sound (drive off)
☐ Distorted Sound (drive on)

Track 39

Sin - gle notes, then Chord! Chord! Chord!    Play it right, you won't get bored.

Ev - en time is ver - y good.    Al - ways play it like you should.

# Pumpkin Song

Play this song with and without distortion. Which do you like better?

☐ Clean Sound (drive off)
☐ Distorted Sound (drive on)

Track 40

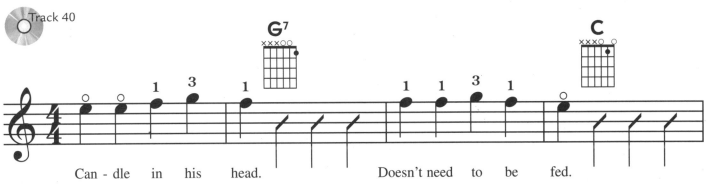

G⁷　　　　　　　　　　　　　　　　C

Can - dle in his head.　　　Doesn't need to be fed.

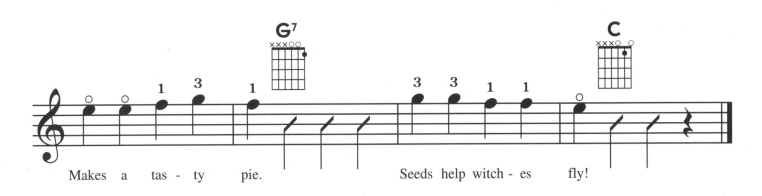

G⁷　　　　　　　　　　　　　　　C

Makes a tas - ty pie.　　　Seeds help witch - es fly!

33

# Notes on the Second String
# Introducing B

Open B

**Hear this note!**
Track 41

A note on the middle line of the staff is called B. Play the 2nd string open.

1st fret

2nd fret

3rd fret

Track 42

**B Warm-up**

# Two Open Strings

Track 43

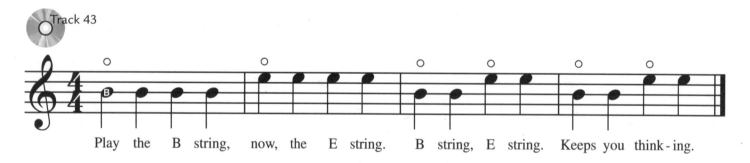

Play the B string, now, the E string. B string, E string. Keeps you think-ing.

# Two-String Melody

Track 44

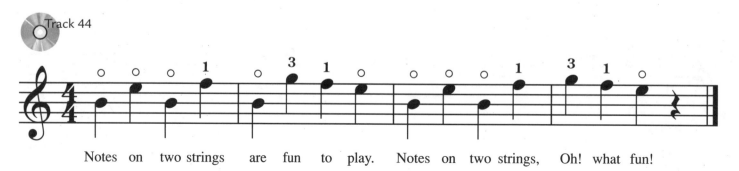

Notes on two strings are fun to play. Notes on two strings, Oh! what fun!

# Jumping Around

Play this song with and without distortion. Which do you like better?

☐ Clean Sound (drive off)
☐ Distorted Sound (drive on)

Track 45

G⁷  G  G⁷                    C

Bounc-ing, bounc-ing,  up  and  down.    Jump-ing, jump-ing,  all  a - round.

G⁷  G  G⁷                    C

In  the  sky, then  on  the  ground.    First you're lost  and  then you're found!

35

# Notes on the Second String
# Introducing C

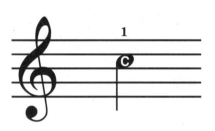
Track 46

A note on the third space of the staff is called C. Use finger 1 to press the 2nd string at the 1st fret. Pick only the 2nd string.

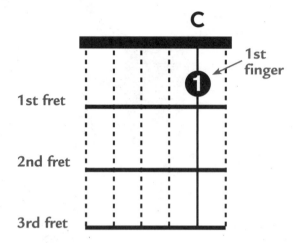

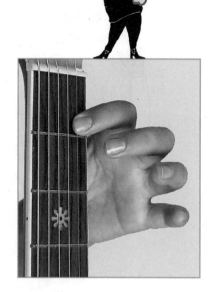

Track 47

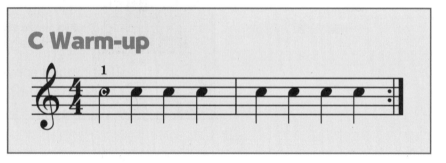

C Warm-up

# Ping Pong Song

Track 48

O - pen B string, first fin - ger C, down to B then up to C.

# Soccer Game

Track 49

Hold

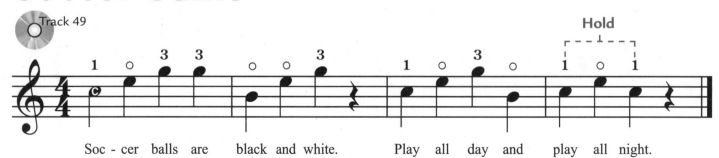

Soc - cer balls are black and white. Play all day and play all night.

36

# The Half Rest

## Introducing the Half Rest

This rest means do not play for two beats, which is the same as 𝄽 𝄽.

Track 50

## Clap and Count out Loud

| | | | | | | (rest) | (rest) | | | (rest) | | (rest) | (rest) | (rest) | | |
1   2   3   4   1   2   (3)   (4)   1   (2)   3   (4)   (1)   (2)   3   4

## Practice Tip

Notice that the note C and the $D^7$ chord are both fingered with finger 1 at the 1st fret on the 2nd string.

In "When I Feel Best," hold the 1st finger down from the third beat of measure 1 until the last beat of measure 5.

Note C

D7 Chord

# When I Feel Best

Track 51

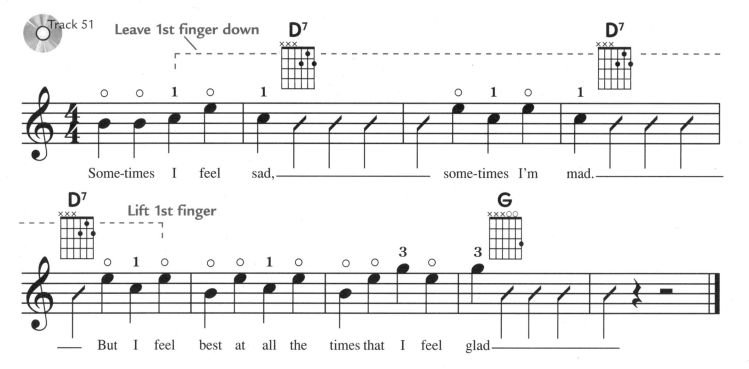

Some-times I feel sad,_____ some-times I'm mad._____

—— But I feel best at all the times that I feel glad——

37

# Notes on the Second String
# Introducing D

**Hear this note!**
Track 52

A note on the fourth line of the staff is called D. Use finger 3 to press the 2nd string at the 3rd fret. Pick only the 2nd string.

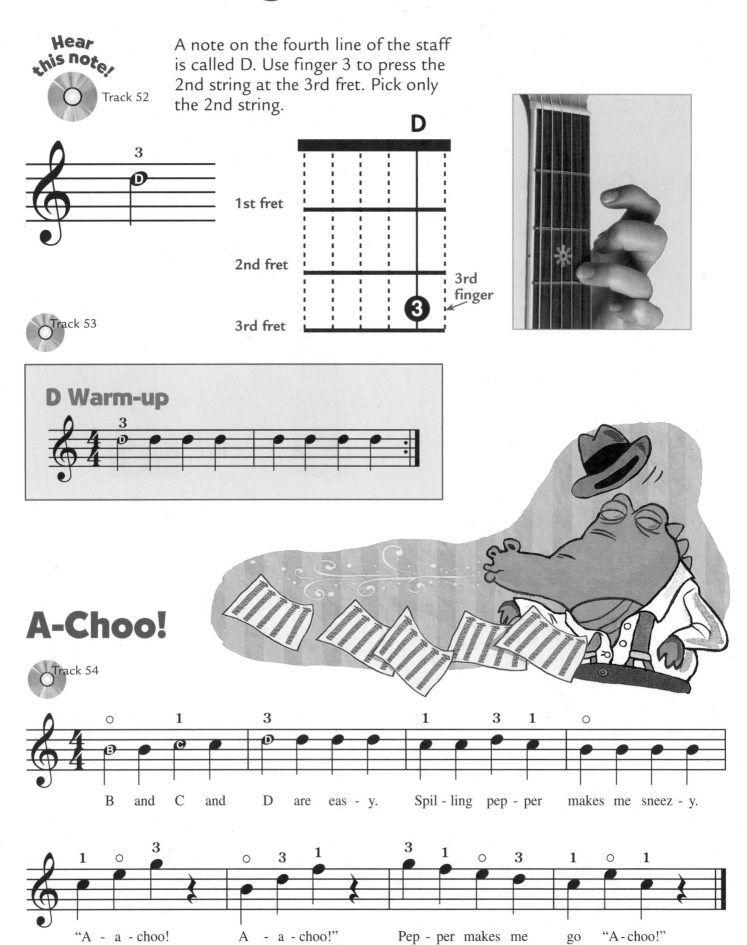

**D**

1st fret

2nd fret

3rd fret

3rd finger

Track 53

**D Warm-up**

# A-Choo!

Track 54

B and C and D are eas - y. Spil - ling pep - per makes me sneez - y.

"A - a - choo! A - a - choo!" Pep - per makes me go "A-choo!"

38

# The Half Note

## Introducing the Half Note

This note lasts two beats.
It is twice as long as a quarter note.

2 beats

Track 55

## Clap and Count out Loud

Play this song with
and without distortion.
Which do you like better?

☐ Clean Sound (drive off)
☐ Distorted Sound (drive on)

# Ode to Joy
## from Beethoven's 9th Symphony

Track 56

**Ludwig van Beethoven**

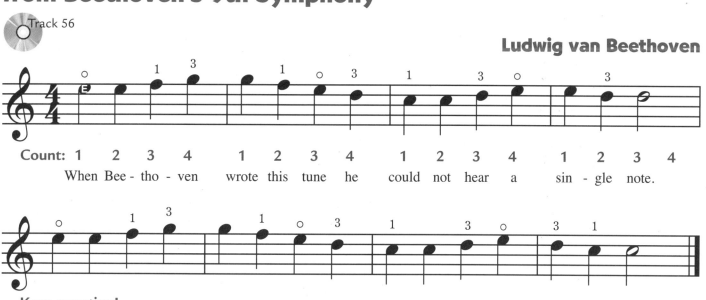

Count: 1  2  3  4   1  2  3  4   1  2  3  4   1  2  3  4

When Bee - tho - ven  wrote this tune  he  could not hear  a  sin - gle note.

**Keep counting!**

But his mus - ic  is  so  awe - some  peo - ple  still  love  things  he  wrote.

# Jingle Bells

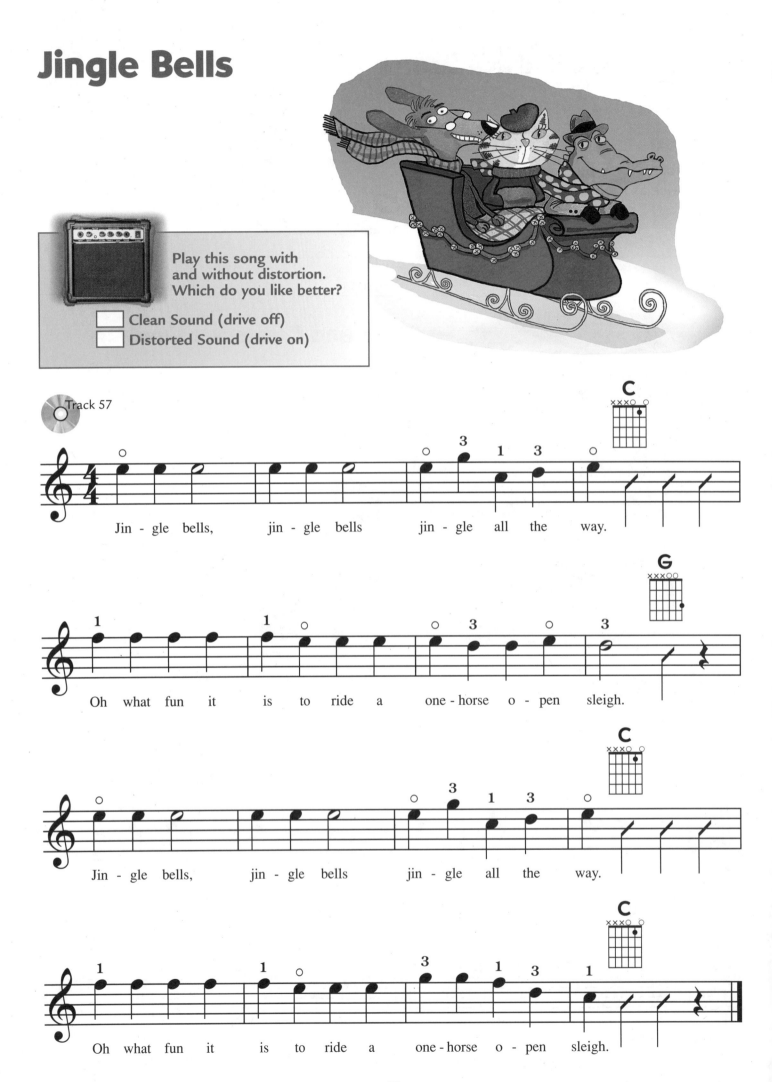

Play this song with and without distortion. Which do you like better?

☐ Clean Sound (drive off)
☐ Distorted Sound (drive on)

Track 57

**C**

Jin - gle bells,    jin - gle bells    jin - gle all the way.

**G**

Oh what fun it    is    to ride    a    one - horse o - pen sleigh.

**C**

Jin - gle bells,    jin - gle bells    jin - gle all the way.

**C**

Oh what fun it    is    to ride    a    one - horse o - pen sleigh.

# Mary Had a Little Lamb

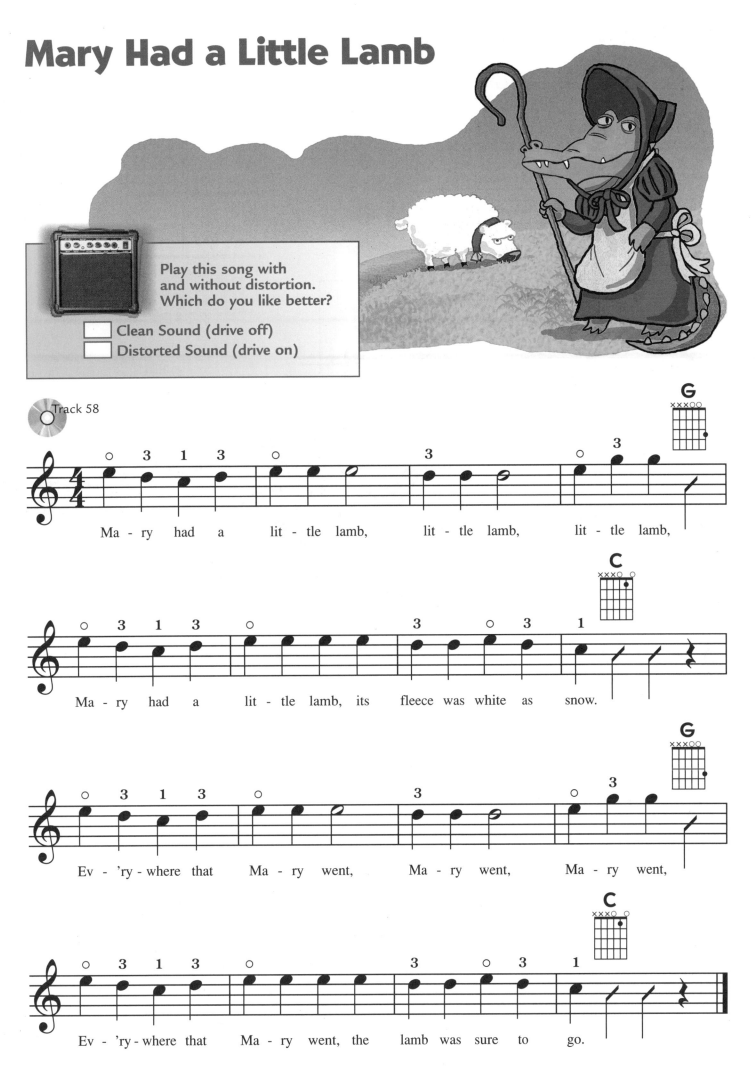

Play this song with
and without distortion.
Which do you like better?

☐ Clean Sound (drive off)
☐ Distorted Sound (drive on)

Track 58

**G**

Ma - ry had a lit - tle lamb, lit - tle lamb, lit - tle lamb,

**C**

Ma - ry had a lit - tle lamb, its fleece was white as snow.

**G**

Ev - 'ry - where that Ma - ry went, Ma - ry went, Ma - ry went,

**C**

Ev - 'ry - where that Ma - ry went, the lamb was sure to go.

# Notes on the Third String
# Introducing G

**Hear this note!**

Track 59

Track 60

A note on the second line of the staff is called G. Pick the 3rd string open.

G
o ← Open

## G Warm-up

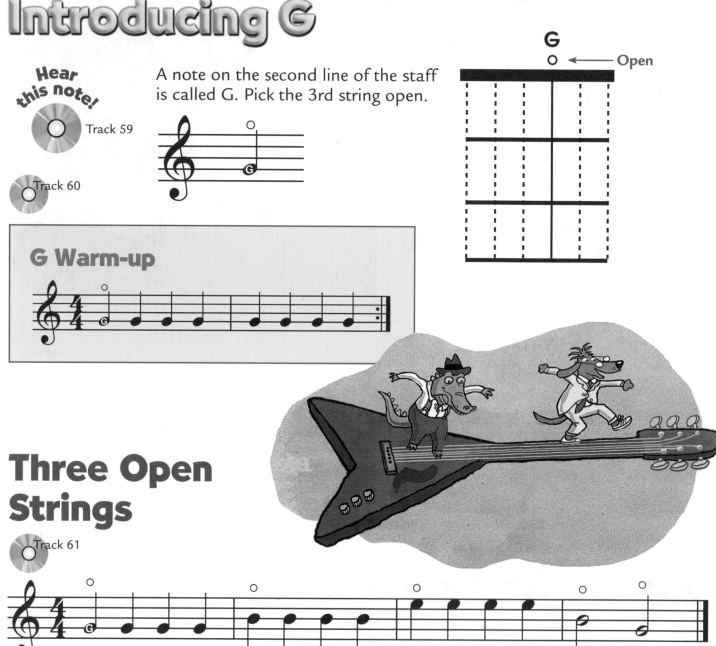

# Three Open Strings

Track 61

Play G o - pen, play B o - pen, play E o - pen, B, G!

# Little Steps and Big Leaps

Track 62

Play - ing on three strings lets me play notes far a - part.

Lit - tle steps and big leaps make my play - ing like fine art.

42

43

# Notes on the Third String
# Introducing A

**Hear this note!**

Track 64

A note on the second space of the staff is called A. Use finger 2 to press the 3rd string at the 2nd fret. Pick only the 3rd string.

**A**

2nd finger → ②

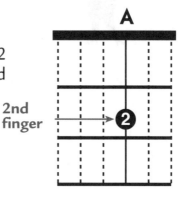

Track 65

## A Warm-up

## Introducing the Whole Note

This note lasts four beats. It is as long as two half notes, or four quarter notes.

𝅝 4 beats

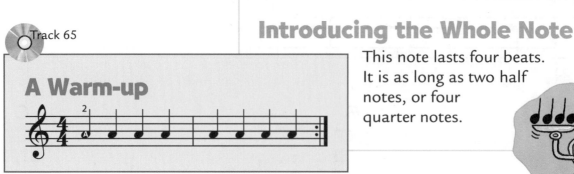

Track 66 **Clap and Count out Loud**

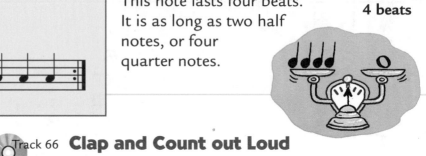

# A Is Easy! Track 67

A is eas-y if you place your sec-ond fin-ger on the G string.

# Taking a Walk Track 68

Walk-ing up to D, then walk down to G.

**D⁷**

**G**

Then I add some chords so I don't get bored.

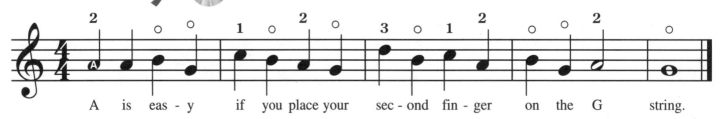

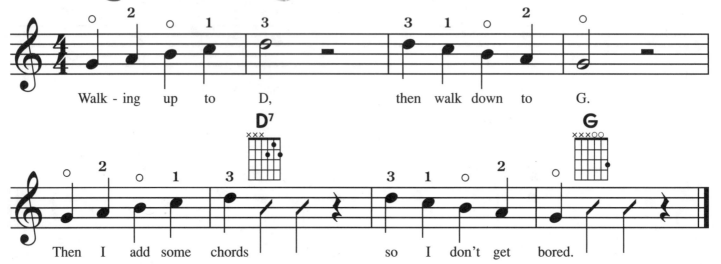

# Aura Lee

Elvis Presley recorded this folk song as a pop ballad called "Love Me Tender."

Play this song with and without distortion. Which do you like better?

☐ Clean Sound (drive off)
☐ Distorted Sound (drive on)

Track 69

1. As the black-bird in the spring 'neath the wil-low tree,
2. sat and piped I heard him sing, sing of Au-ra Lee!

Au-ra Lee! Au-ra Lee! Maid of gold-en hair,

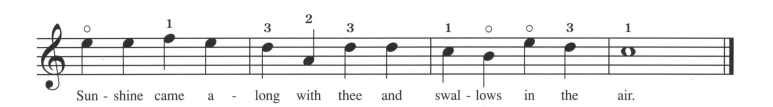

Sun-shine came a-long with thee and swal-lows in the air.

# She'll Be Comin' 'Round the Mountain

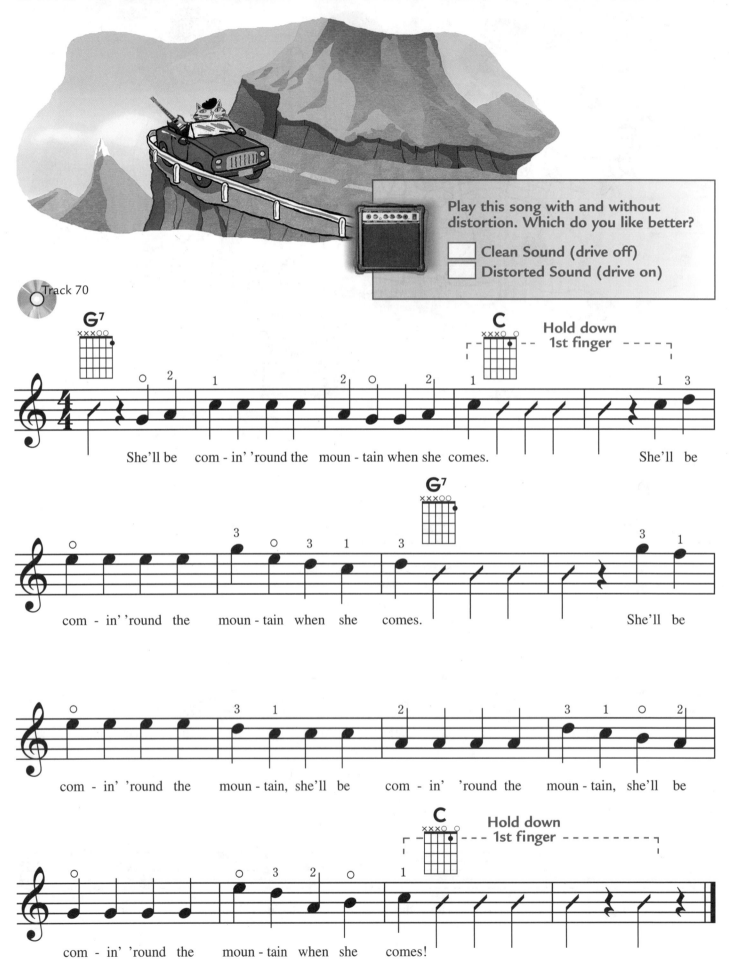

Play this song with and without distortion. Which do you like better?

☐ Clean Sound (drive off)
☐ Distorted Sound (drive on)

Track 70

She'll be com-in' 'round the moun-tain when she comes. She'll be

com-in' 'round the moun-tain when she comes. She'll be

com-in' 'round the moun-tain, she'll be com-in' 'round the moun-tain, she'll be

com-in' 'round the moun-tain when she comes!

# Music Matching Games

## Chords

Draw a line to match each chord frame on the left to the correct photo on the right.

1.

2.

3.

4.

## Symbols

Draw a line to match each symbol on the left to its name on the right.

1. 𝅝          **Treble clef**

2.          **Quarter note**

3.          **Whole note**

4.          **Quarter slash**

5.          **Half note**

6.          **Double bar line**

7.          **Half rest**

8.          **Repeat sign**

9.          **Quarter rest**

## Notes

Draw a line to match each note on the left to its correct music notation on the right.

1.

2.

3.

4.

5.

6.

7.

8.

## Answer Key

**Chords**
1: page 10; 2: page 12; 3: page 16; 4: page 20

**Symbols**
1: page 44; 2: page 39; 3: page 25; 4: page 8;
5: page 25; 6: page 18; 7: page 37; 8: page 11;
9: page 8

**Notes**
1: page 26; 2: page 29; 3: page 30; 4: page 34;
5: page 36; 6: page 38; 7: page 42; 8: page 44

# Certificate of Promotion

This certifies that

_____

has mastered and perfected

Book 1 of Alfred's Kid's Electric Guitar Course

and is hereby promoted into

Book 2 of Alfred's Kid's Electric Guitar Course

_____
Teacher / Parent

_____
Date